LIVING WAGES

Also by Michael Chitwood

POETRY

Salt Works (1992)

Whet (1995)

The Weave Room (1998)

Gospel Road Going (2002)

From Whence (2007)

Spill (2007)

Poor-Mouth Jubilee (2010).

ESSAYS

Hitting Below the Bible Belt: Baptist Voodoo, Blood Kin, Grandma's Teeth, and Other Stories from the South (1998)

Finishing Touches (2006)

LIVING WAGES

POEMS

MICHAEL
CHITWOOD

TUPELO PRESS

NORTH ADAMS
MASSACHUSETTS

Living Wages.
Copyright © 2014 Michael Chitwood. All rights reserved.

Library of Congress Cataloging-in-Publication Data
Chitwood, Michael.
[Poems. Selections]
Living wages : poems / Michael Chitwood. -- First edition.
    pages ; cm
ISBN 978-1-936797-48-6 (pbk. : alk. paper)
I. Title.
PS3553.H535A6 2014
811'.54--dc23

                                        2014025764

Cover and text designed by Josef Beery.
Text set in Monotype Baskerville, a digitized version of the 1923 Monotype metal
type based on the 18th-century type created by Englishman, John Baskerville.

Cover photograph by Lydia Chitwood. This wood plane belonged to
Trobie Washington Chitwood, Sr., and was used in the crafting of many
handsome pieces of furniture.

Paperback original, first edition: October 2014.

Tupelo Press
P.O. Box 1767, 243 Union Street, Loft 305
North Adams, Massachusetts 01247
Telephone: (413) 664–9611 / editor@tupelopress.org
www.tupelopress.org

Tupelo Press is an award-winning independent literary press that publishes fine
fiction, nonfiction, and poetry in books that are a joy to hold as well as read.
Tupelo Press is a registered 501(c)(3) nonprofit organization, and we rely on
public support to carry out our mission of publishing extraordinary work that
may be outside the realm of large commercial publishers. Financial donations are
welcome and are tax deductible.

ART WORKS.
arts.gov

Supported in part by an award from
the National Endowment for the Arts

FOR LYDIA

"I know you, you know me."

Contents

Notch

Guides and Stops

The Stairs

The stairs are neither going up nor coming down.
This could be done if done slowly.
She puts the left foot down and then the right,
coming to rest on each step, each little stage.
Ah, she has arrived again on this small platform.
She grips the rail with her left hand,
the palm of her right hand flat on the close wall.
The stairway is really a hallway.
So many times she has gone down and come up.
This could be done if done slowly.
And carried: In the early days one foot to each step,
the skirt flouncing, a list in her head,
the jar to get, the jar of summer caught
in its own steeped syrup.
What was it she wanted now,
each step a pause?

Children. She had heard them overhead,
their quick scuttle when she had clothes to move,
the little bodies of the clothes
returned again and again up the stairs
into the everyday heaven to be dirtied.
This could be done if done slowly,
easing down, the cool musk rising to her,
and each step a rest,
each one a chance to catch her breath,
to steady and study ankle and wrist,
those necessary narrows,
how many times had she passed through,
taken down and brought up?

This could be done if done slowly,
the hitch and get along, the small-time arriving-at
learned through years,
the saved, the preserved,
glass jars with their goods like lanterns aglow,
this could be done.

Amen to the Ax

I would venture that she never said a prayer in her life.

But she made a chocolate pie worth praying over.

She once cleared a hillside of pines after her boy went into the service.

She had hats with feathers and shells. Feral things that mated once a
year, yowling and spitting.

She lit long matches.

She went to church because that's what people did.

She cut the pines with an ax. The tattoo would have been audible at a
quarter mile. To a listening ear.

After my wife met her, my wife said, "Why didn't you tell me she
was obese?"

I said, "I'd never noticed."

She once shot a cat for nearly tripping her.

She wore glasses and kept false teeth in a cupboard.

Doctors delighted her.

She said she had heavy bones.

Which may have accounted for her not owning a swimsuit. And the
  business with prayer.

She tried to drive once and knocked the porch askew from the house.

The pines reseeded. As children we played among their shadows,
  happy days full of meaningless shouts.

Purchased from Morris Furniture Company with a Year's Savings

The legs were like hers,
thick, thigh and calf,
if you could call them that,
about the same size,
but the feet were claws
clutching orbs that rested
on the buckling linoleum.
A waxy tablecloth,
and always a basket,
with a white cloth that covered
cold biscuits.
How many mornings with a knife
and a pan of apples or peaches
did she unscroll the skins
like silent sentences, long,
vowel-ripe, red and blush?
The station-wagon man
would come and sit
with his samples of Rawleigh products
she might have need of
this afternoon visit, once a month.
And children, two, three,
tablets spread, thick purple pencils,
tongue tips pink in concentration,
book-bound, alphabet-snagged
to the tabletop.
Such complaining.

And hunger.
Before the clatter of fork
and spoon and bowl,
a pause, the home-from-work baritone
repeating, always the same,
We ask this in Thy name
so that to the children
it was like a song
learned in a foreign language,
just sound, the daily sound
before dark and dreams,
and then the meal.

The Call

There was the rumor
of a deep night/early morning
secret train that a crew
had to be called in for,
and they got double time
for their trouble. Big money.
They cleared the tracks,
put everything on the side rails,
even the coal cars that were priority.
And when it left the yard
with only three cars
and a puller and a pusher,
jimmy-john scooting
before it was out of sight.
Everyone had a theory:
Some millionaire had a coupe
shipped to Norfolk from Europe
and wanted it in New York by the weekend.
Or the government needed a rocket
pronto to Fort Meade. Or gold—
gold was always a good bet.
No one ever knew for sure
or knew anyone who had been on the crew,
but when the call came,
and it would come, it would,
why sure, sure, you'd go,
that kind of money and all.

Handle

We were trying to re-hang a door
on the little shed he used
for the push mower and gas cans.
Actually, "the shed" was a camper shell
that fit his old pickup
which he sold but kept the shell
because he kept everything
in case he could use it again,
which usually led to aggravation,
as this was becoming,
because to use it again
required some modification, some change
or repair after lack of use.
Isn't it odd that use is what keeps a hinge vital,
which is what we were trying to repair,
or he was. I was six or seven,
distracted by a bee,
and not holding the door in place
so he could get the screws set
which made him grab the door
and yell, "Like this, just hold it here.
Is that so hard?"
In those days, he flew off the handle quickly:
the handle of the tool of trying to repair
things around the house,
the patch job that always looked patched,
temporary, taped, propped, until it really broke.
In those days, I was no help,
not interested in anything other than cartoons
or imaginary stories I created

while riding my bike in circles in the driveway.
In those days, I had no inkling,
no idea of the flying-off-the-handle nature
of having watched your father die
and looking at your inattentive son
and knowing that he will watch you.

Repair

Here we are again.
The timing is off in the Country Sedan
station wagon. Dad is out of his white shirt
and into his blue coveralls and cap.
He says I'll have to hold the light.
It's fall and dark after supper
and cold, my breath like the exhaust
from the tailpipe when he cranks the car.
The light is the one with the long yellow cord
that says, "Heavy Duty."
The bulb is caught in a trap,
a tin shield on one side
and a grid of bars on the other.
The bulb is like a bird in a cage,
the hawk I saw once at a roadside zoo
that had only seven animals.
"Hold the light so I can see," my father says.
The hawk had yellow and black eyes
and was motionless inside the cage.
On a branch, he was big at the top and small at the bottom,
"Hold the light on what I'm doing,"
and only his eyes moved, a flicker, but you could feel him,
you could almost hear a buzz like the tiny wire in the bulb.
The grid of the cage is all that's keeping the bulb
from unfolding its shining wings and springing off its perch.
"Here." My father grabs my hands and positions them
in the air above the engine. "Now don't move."
Both hands in the air clasp the neck of the light;
my arms ache. The hawk is heavy. He's eaten

an entire black snake. I can feel it in him, the thick
crawling muscles digesting.
"Please, please, hold the light. Hold it still."
My father's engine runs rougher.
He doesn't know how heavy the hawk is.
He only wants the light where he needs it.
But the light is burning in my arms now.
They throb with it. The light is draining into me
and that's why he can't see.
My hands and forearms are warm because the light
is seeping into them. The yellow light of the hawk's eyes
inside my forearms is turning red,
the red you see when you close your eyes
after looking directly into a bright bare bulb.
This is my father's light,
bright now in my dark.

The Elements Will Have Their Way

1

The water did not want to be in the bucket.
Where was I going, so long ago?
The water leapt, dove over the side of the bucket.
Why did the water not want to be carried?
Where did it want to go that it was not going?
The bucket's thin handle cut into my hand.
My hand wanted to refuse the handle.
The water bucked and made the bucket bang my knee.
The water jumped to me, darkened my clothes.
Where was I going with this quarrelsome water?
What spirit it had. It would not be held.
It held my hand reluctantly. It sloshed and tugged.
It glupped and knocked against the bucket.
It was hard-headed water that would not lie down.
I leaned away from it, my head cocked in the pull.
What would this water do, forced to go the way I went?

2

Men were running. Men that I had never seen run before
were running. The fire was going where it wanted to go.
The fire went in four directions. No, five:
Up too. It climbed trees, a bright, hot child.
The men beat at the fire on the ground with brooms
and wide rakes. The tines of the rakes sang
like harps. The notes of the music were sparks.
The fire swayed and dodged the men.
When they smacked at the fire, it jumped.
Where the fire wanted to be was away from the men

and the men wanted it with them, wanted it close
but that is not what the fire wanted. It was wild to run.

3

The wind made the trees look like cattle
shivering their hides to keep off flies.
The wind aged the surface of the water;
all in an instant it wrinkled.
The wind sabled the long grass
in the field that would be mown later.
But for now the wind stroked the pelt of the field.
The wind found the gleam of the grass,
the white beneath the green, the sheen.
The wind ran its hand over the fur of the field
as if for the sake of that velvet feeling.

Later, in the night, the wind came against the house
in gusts that thudded and rattled the plate shelves.
Tree limbs cracked like rifle shots. The train of the wind
roared by. Its dark, invisible freight was late, terribly late.

4

Some small clods of dirt rolled back into the hole.
They hopped down the slope of the pile the machine made.
The machine's one arm reached again and again
into the hole and curled to scoop a bucket full
and rose and swung to the side to uncurl
over the peaked pile and let fall dirt on dirt.
Some of it tumbled down the pile's side

almost as if it were unwilling to be dug,
not ready to leave its place in the ground
to make this square hole that would be refilled later
but not with as much dirt, and this dirt did not
want to be the part that would be left out.

Finish Work

Of his table saw I will speak,
but not his wood plane
displayed now on my bookshelf,
its shape too elegant, its cut too precise.

~

A male cardinal has come
to my windowsill.
Over and over he thrashes
against the glass,
battering his own enemy reflection.

~

He worked in a small shed out back,
dust climbing the sun slats.

~

During mating season
the finches' butter yellow brightens to sunburst,
once a year.

~

He was a furniture maker in his day job too,
mostly for Bald Knob Furniture in the days before safety regs.
He was missing the ends of eight of his fingers.
When he took me to Moran's Store to get a Brownie,
a cold chocolate drink,
he would hold my hand as we walked across the parking lot.
What I felt was what wasn't there.

~

In his hand, a boat,
sailing across creation.
That's near to breaking my vow.

~

He made a bedroom suite for my parents,
chest of drawers, vanity, night stand,
and, of course, the bed.
All walnut, rich, dark, fine-grained wood.

~

My father was an only child.
I first heard the phrase as lonely child.

~

I picture the wood curls at his feet
as he worked,
blonde locks of a beautiful woman.

~

During mating season,
our suburban deer herd goes crazy.
A buck crashes through the plate glass
of a downtown shop.
Does slam into cars in their headlong flight
running from bucks.

~

He breathed his creations,
inhaled the fine blonde dust.
Then he'd go out to the overturned bucket
and put fire to the Lucky Strikes.

~

I don't know why she felt she needed to tell me.
I can still see the curve of the off ramp we were on.
I can feel the centrifugal shove the curve gave the car.
It was the middle of the trip.
We'd been talking about nothing much,
just the two of us.
"Your grandfather cheated on me."

~

What he made in his spare time,
his pieces, grace many houses, homes.
Even mine.

~

A pair of cardinals at the feeder,
he, scarlet, selects a sunflower seed
and feeds it to her, drab olive, sitting beside him.

~

In his mind, before he even began,
he knew where everything went.

~

He, third grade education. She, seventh.
In the days before birth control was common
or ever discussed, an only child.
When Granddad died they had been married 38 years.

~

Before he made the first piece,
he made the table saw,
its guides and stops.

~

We, the three grandchildren, took turns picking what we wanted
after Grandmother died.
I took a little cedar chest he had made.
She had saved letters in it.
There was one from my dad, not sure the occasion.
In part it read, "Mother, I'll take your hand and Dad's
and hold us together."
I wonder how many pieces were already missing from that hand.

~

Grain. It continues,
does not end where the piece has been cut.
You have to understand that.

Snug, square, trig, true,
As far as I know he made only one bed.

~

Dust climbing the sun slats,
the ache of that.

~

The bed was in the spare room at my parents'.
It was where my grandmother stayed when she became ill.
She died there.

~

He'd run his hand along a finish to know that it was done.

Where I'm Coming From

the room where the pale roots soaked in pie tins
where Jesus and John Kennedy hububbed

tobacco was hoed, suckered, primed,
a pony was used to terrify two small girls

the room where whatnots crowded the corners
and what nots were reviewed every payday

where he came home without some finger tips
taken by the saws that were never seen

one stub was poked into the small of her back
and "get what you're going to get and let's go" was said

every Christmas for 25 years after it was said
the first time and that stub pushed in the back like a gun barrel

the room where the TV snowed and one chest of drawers
was all a little girl got out of an auction

her parents dead with the influenza, siblings too,
and she was uncle-placed upon the chest of drawers

and no one would bid for it, her throne,
and so it came to rest in the room off the room

where a Bible was writ with the gospel of names
the gospel of here-before-us-blood

who knocked and hacked and stomped snow from boots
and hung out sheets pinked with birth

and kneaded and knotted, knuckled ears
in church where God banged hard in the upright

and men smoked unfiltereds afterward by the stoop
the room itself Lucky Strike struck, white sock propped

after shotgunned squirrels were parboiled and fried,
the room whose timbers were 2x4s

and the wind wrinkled the aluminum hide
around the room incensed by the battered percolator

its top knob throbbed early with the tannic sap
and cooked all day rendering its brew by evening

to something you could almost chew
the room rampant with the unspoken

the aforementioned unmentioned
wrestlers grappling in the snow the only crowing

the room where warts were spoken to and made to vanish
an asfidity bag was recommended to be worn

and the assurance was made that the Lord could be counted on
to be counted on for however what turned out turned out.

Making It So

The Collection

Even two years later, she still gets correspondence
addressed to him. Correspondence. This like that.

Mostly about his hobby. Coin collector brochures.
Announcements of collector swap meets. His pastime.

A way to spend an afternoon back when an afternoon
needed spending. Before all the silence flooded the house.

He had old currency. Nickels worth ten dollars.
And heavy, the bags. Musical, too.

She needs to sort through them all.
That's what she should do, realize its value.

But what she is thinking of is spending it,
buying gum and soft drinks, maybe a chocolate bar.

Just get face value for mint-condition rarities.
Get them back into circulation. Circulation. The afterlife

where someone else could get them as change
and be joyful at the luck of finding his life's pleasure.

The Clatter of Aluminum Ladders

Something's being painted or patched.
The rattle of the handy, portable
rack of stairs is a sound like no other.
The shudder of the extension,
as one reach rides its twin
up until it's twice as long as it began.
Good work needs good assistance
and what a clever commotion this is.
And light, for what it does.
One man can haul it in
then send it to the second story.
Its warped old wooden brethren
could perform no such trick. They were
a single rickety climb with rounded
rungs that left ghost pressure in the feet
and went about their silent jobs
without anyone being the wiser,
and higher was imagination's work.

Making Time

He could make a day
of burning a pile of leaves.
Raking first, to the bare spot
at the side of the yard.
Letting the damp undersides
dry a while,
he might go inside
and put some dry beans on to soak;
whatever he did inside,
no one was sure.
Then the lighting,
just one spot, a thread of smoke
and the rest of the day,
nudging, lifting the smudgy hem
to let a little air in,
to keep the smolder,
leaning on the rake, shepherd-like
and looking around, a cloud,
the ground around the pile,
the bare tree limbs.
Now and again,
a spurt of flame sprang up,
yellow elf.
What color did he see
when he saw yellow
with time passing, watching,
being watched,
the little fire working
spark and flare?

The Ways of the Lord

Mothers blew smoke
into the ears of their children
to ease the ache.
That was the power of God,
the incense of tobacco,
that crop that paid the mortgage.
This was a healing that caused cancer
and put food on the table.
Say what you will
they were good times, those dying afternoons
when we tied hand after hand
of gold leaf.
Coffin nails, some called the cigs
but God had a plan
for each plant.
Early in the morning
working in the fields was like swimming
in the dew-drenched fronds, cool and wet,
and the dark tar of the resin
made every touch
a latching on.

Sweeping

A meal was not complete
until she had pulled out the chairs
and swept under the table
and by the stove.

~

He rode with his father
because the older kids kissed
at the back of the bus,
which smelled of others' lunches,
so he got to school early
when only the grizzled janitor was there,
and he had spread red sawdust in the halls
and swept with a wide broom.
The boy walked in the broom path
to his classroom and listened
to the hiss-hiss of the broom's kiss.

~

When the others had put away
their cards and jokes and gripes
and the unsaid things
they came each week not to say
and the cars had crunched from the gravel lot,
he went to the closet
and got the big horse-bristle pusher
and gave the place a once over,
then felt OK to turn off the lights

and give the knob a jiggle
to make sure it was locked.

~

The prancing horses had been combed to a sheen
and the ramrod uniformed riders' boots glistened,
swords clicking against saddles.
In the wake of the parade
they came with the wide-mouthed shovels
and the sturdy long-handled brooms
to scoop up the horses' droppings.

~

While some of the ladies checked
the undersides of casserole dishes
for the taped-on name of the owner
and others finished wiping the tables,
and "they took it well" and
"he's better off" was said once more,
two would work from the walls
to the center of the fellowship hall
before getting the dust pans.

~

Once, when she was a girl
on a family trip in her father's new car
with the rich smell of melon and leather,
she saw an old woman
in the dirt yard of a shack
moving as though waltzing a stick

and the orderly stroke marks of the dance
all around the sagging house.

~

He would only go out at dusk,
the coastal sun too fierce in the day.
He wore dress wingtips,
khakis and a button-down shirt
but walked every evening
and paused and faced the surf crash,
hands behind his back
until it was too dark, even for him,
to see the other side,
so later we didn't mind
sweeping up the little piles of sand
that spilled from his shoes.

~

Last thing,
after they'd gotten the body settled
in its cushioned rest and the clothes adjusted,
the director would take the whisk
and lightly brush, more for the ritual
than any lingering dust.

~

No meal was complete,
the broom's sound a cross
between scissors and sigh.

Cleaning

The women, smelling of coffee,
come on Wednesday
and tickle the cross
with a feather duster
and speak of colic
and the wanting of less month
and more paycheck,
and when they leave
with their rags and sprays
and the damp mops of their industry,
they are not disturbed by the shadow
passing along the ground
and do not look up,
for there is more to do.

The Patterns

"Saying will not make it so,"
I remember her saying
to something I said
without turning her head from her work.
Her case knives weighted a dress pattern.
The pattern was like parchment,
a gospel to be cut from or cut out
in the shape of her knowing how
to bring it together
and change it to fit
the one it was made for.
She pedaled the machine to work the needle;
its jumping knit the seams.
She could have been making a girl
with that antique contraption, making it sew.
All the while she was not trusting language
but making, Butterick pattern after pattern
and altering, a little taken in here,
a little let out there
because each body she made for
did not exactly fit the pattern
and she allowed for that,
did it by eye.

Raking

From a distance, you might think
I'm practicing ballroom here in my yard,
dance being the gathering of motion
into an order. The sweeping moves
pull through the arms and shoulders
and from the trunk too, the body's core.
I've made a neat pile.

And then the wind, the leaves' other partner,
comes and swirls them, making its own music
for a dance, dance being the release of order
into motion, the light touch of the hand
to the small of the back, the leaves unstacking
in turns and steps across the yard,
precise randomness, scatter's two-step.

Another Dollar

It's 8 a.m. and the tradesmen are gearing up.
The electrician straps on his belt,
gar-snouted pliers, the crimp, the volt meter.
Masons heft their mortarboards.
They cymbal their trowels together
just for the sound, the clean blades.
The carpenter has holstered his hammer.

You, who do not have tackle,
take in hand such handle as you have.
Feel the polish of its grip, its balance
in that plumb moment before work begins.

Shovels

To Start the Day

Every morning,
coughing and sputtering,
gargling his phlegm up,
he sounded like one of his old trucks
trying to start
and then he'd fart, the backfire.

That was the job,
the cold start-up, getting to lunch,
then ditching through the afternoon,
laying the water pipe.
"Every day digging the grave," he'd say,
taking a break from the backhoe,
"but it's a living."
You do it for a day.
Then you do it again.

The Backhoe

after EB's "The Bight"

The creaking arm reaches for another scoop of earth.
The yellow tractor body is braced on its jacks,
back tires lifted
so that it looks like a man in a stance,
feet planted for a heavy pull.
And it does pull,
bucket after bucket of dirt
clawed from the ground.
The operator seems in a drowse. His arms
are easy at the levers that guide the big arm.
He's done this so many days
his muscles know the motion
and the hydraulic boom makes a smooth curl
as if it was the man's own limb. The ditch unfills.
Some kid might see a scorpion
with its jointed tail stinging the earth.
This is a job. There's a sandwich at noon.
It's tight between the buildings.
The tractor chuffs and edges;
the trench skirts foundations,
grave-sheer, mud-slick walls shining.
What's done must be undone to be complete,
the fresh-turned earth a scar but fragrant.

Altar

A work-day Adam had given names
to all the grades of rock—
Crusher Run for the sandy gravel
that packed to make driveways,
Terra Rosa for the decorative beds,
and Rip-Rap for the football-sized stones
we stacked along the shoreline
to keep it from washing.
You had to unload the Rip-Rap
by hand from the backhoe bucket.
It was too expensive to dump
and risk rolling into the lake.
It made music like a wind chime
when you chinked it into place.
Placing rock on rock,
what older human act?
Sometimes the truck's run to the quarry
took longer than usual
and there was nothing to do but wait,
toss a few pebbles into the lake,
think what you could only think
while waiting for rocks with names.

Flip

There are miracles in this world
but they are working-class, Wednesday morning miracles
that go mostly unnoticed by the priests.
We towed the air compressor for the drill
behind a better-days pickup
and were on the way to shoot some rock
where they were digging the basement for a lake house.
The secondary road was mined with potholes,
the truck's suspension stiff as a bed frame.
We probably forgot the safety bolt
so on a big bounce the compressor tongue
jumped from the hitch and speared the asphalt.
The safety chains snapped,
jerking the bumper
a half foot from the truck bed.
The compressor, that piano-sized chug monster,
somersaulted in the air
and landed back on its wheels
rocking to the roadside as though we had parked it there.
And there was nothing to do but shake our heads
and hitch it back up and go drill the shot holes
for a house some swell
would read cooking magazines in.

Lull

It was clay pipe joints for sewer line,
cast iron for water, but either way
you had to roll them into the harness
and catch a chain link in the hook
so the backhoe could haul them to the trench.
Same motions, rolling the pipe with your foot,
closing the harness, catching the chain,
which made it killingly dangerous, the inattention.
When the hoe first hoisted the pipe
it would swing wildly like a drunk
conducting a band, the joint the backhoe's baton
rampaging through the music.
How could we forget that even after they settled down
and we were slow walking them
with a hand in the flared end that coupled with the next joint,
that if the hoe lurched or the driver jerked
they could swing and bash our brains to mush?
But as the afternoon wore on, cicadas grinding,
the sleepiness we packed in our lunch buckets
made us believe, though we walked with sudden death,
it was just a few dollars-worth of doing,
burying pipe, and we would go home after.

Blast Mat

The blast mat was made of old tires,
cut in half and strung on steel cable,
all those trips—to Iowa, the grocery,
the hospital, an orchard in the fall—
cinched together like a bracelet of travel,
and the bracelets, six of them,
were joined with more cable to make the mat.
It took a crane to lift the thing.
We had to drill into the rock,
dog-work with the pneumatic drill,
first the four-foot bit, then the six,
then the eight, grinding the hole deeper into the rock.
You could taste the chalk of the rock dust.
We threaded sticks of dynamite
into the holes, the last one with a blasting cap
and then the frilly wires to the detonator.
The crane operator would drape the mat
over the rock like a blanket on a bed:
with the thump of the blast the mat jumped
but held down the shards and chips,
not much of a fireworks payoff after all that drilling.
But one day the foreman had to go bid a job
and we drilled and loaded the holes.
We were blasting out a foundation
for a house at the lake.
A blistering day and we'd worn
bandanas bandit-style to not breathe the dust,
and when we were ready,
we said, what the hell, no mat, forget it.

We crimped the wires to the detonator
and got behind some trees.
When it went, we heard the shrapnel
nicking the trees and one chunk
the size of a suitcase hurtled
in almost slow-motion catapult
toward a sailboat moored on the lake.
A direct hit would sink the boat sure,
but it ca-choomed to the right side,
water spouting up four or five feet
and all of us releasing the breath we'd held.
A couple came from below deck,
scrambling up, waving and shouting,
and Bill, who most wanted payoff after labor,
shouted back. "Wake up. Wake the hell up."

Relief

Early August and no rain for two weeks.
The dirt at the job site had turned to talc,
puffing up around our boots with every step.
It swirled behind the trucks, billowed
and settled gritty on windshields and dashboards.
We were breathing the earth.
There was talk of getting a water tanker
to at least spray down the truck tracks.
Shovel handles were silty, the pipe joints silky
when we held their flared mouths
as we walked them with the backhoe to the trench.
That fog of dirt was just too much.
When the mongrel came sniffing at tires
and made the mistake of picking Harley for begging
I figured she'd get a boot in the ribs
you could count like stair rails.
Her teats were distended so along with starving
she was trying to feed a brood of pups.
Harley was known to grab up and crack
a snake like a whip so the head popped off.
He once took a dump in a paper bag
and put it in the mailbox of a homeowner
who'd complained about the noise of our equipment.
I thought the dog would get a shovel on the head
and Harley would say he put it out of misery.
But what it got was a sandwich from his lunch box
and some water from the Igloo cooler.
The dust kept swirling, finding its way
into our pockets and even ears

but the dog came back every day
because we all began to feed it
and the dust be damned.

Ricky Can Dance

What I want to know—
but no, I'll ask you tomorrow,

today the winter woods are mottled,
gray, some black, a little white.

I want to know—
but it can wait, a squirrel

is stripping bark from a poplar branch.
Is it trying to get at some food?

Maybe there's a sweet marrow
just under the gray bark.

One summer I worked construction
with a guy named Ricky,

big guy, bushy mustache,
who would bark at every lunch break

"Bean time, eat time, fart time,"
and would open one of the pickup's doors

and switch on the key
and crank up the radio

and we'd have Jagger
getting no satisfaction

or Redding sittin on the dock
of the bay in the mornin sun

with the half shells of starter homes
and half-dug sewer line

we were digging around us.
The homes would become stages

for R&B dramas about debt
and drinking and cheating

and just generally not getting done
what signing the mortgage papers

had promised would get done
in these two-bedroom one-baths

and Ricky would boogaloo
in clay-smeared Red Camel boots,

the truck blaring and the boss
saying he was going to run the battery down

though he never did,
and what I want to know here today is—

but the backhoe is firing up
and it's time to get back

to reading the transit,
keeping right the grade in the ditch

and there will be another day
when I will ask you

and you can tell me the truth
but until then Ricky can dance.

Mud

It rained in the night
and now our boot soles
are getting second soles,
the tacky clay grabbing on,
dancing us in a clumsy Swan Lake
of holding and letting go

and it's got Ricky
in a mood
as he damns the wet dirt
and says that all the cars
in the Live Your Life 500

will have sponsorship
from Tide, yes, and Shout
but also Jinx Funeral Home,
with the Helping Hand on the hood
and the fans behind the chain-link

longing for a paint swap
that will end in fire,
a wall rub of an ending,
that everyone waits out a race for.

That's why we go to races, Ricky says,
as he scraps off the mud
with a shovel
and says it ends always
in shovels and dirt

and then grins his Ricky grin and says
but not today, buddy boy,
not today.

Summer Job

At the end of the work day
you could tell exactly how far you had gotten
and how much farther there was to go.
Of course, it was just a ditch for a pipeline
to carry the reeking slop
that a neighborhood of toilets
would slosh together to be drained away
but it was clean, the trench,
the slick walls the backhoe bucket cut
and the precise grade of the bottom.
My job was to sight the transit.
I gave a thumbs up or thumbs down
or the OK sign if the pitch was right
so that some future day shit would flow
just as it should, down hill,
but you knew where you stood,
what you had done in a day,
and what more there was to do
and every meaningful thing I had said
I had said without a word.

The Way of the World

"These sons of bitches," he says.
He's mining the pickup bed, clattering
among the tools.
"These sons of bitches today."
It isn't clear if the tools,
shovels, digging bar, mattock, pick,
are the sons of bitches
and if they are only sons of bitches today
and tomorrow and yesterday not sons of bitches.
"These sons of bitches today, I tell you."
Empty soda cans tossed into the bed
add their rattle to the clamor
of his jerking and tossing aside
on this day with these sons of bitches,
whoever, whatever, they are,
here, all around us,
working their bitchery
as he comes up with the chalk line
with which we will mark and then dig
straight and true
in the presence of all these sons of bitches.

Notch

The Song

I first heard the song
from the treadle of the old sewing machine
as my grandmother pumped it.
She was putting a girl together.
"I'm doing the arms," she said.

But the song gets around:
to the wheels of the IV pole
my father scooted around the hospital corridors.
He was siphoning off another day.

And in that salt-eaten pickup,
its bed piled with mattresses and cardboard boxes,
the hopeful detritus of another move,
as it hauled the song.

The song's scald was in the old file drawers
at the county clerk's,
where deeds and wills, last testaments, were being retrieved.

And now it rides
in the boy's empty, rained-on wagon,
his little load of nothing
that he happily pulls around for hours.

Harvest

Every year now, in autumn, they have a festival:
the Autumn Festival, not Fall.
They gather antique harvesting machinery
with the slapping canvas belts
and the clattering cutter bars,
some with steam engines sighing and hissing.
There are booths with ham biscuits and pie slices
and haybale benches and usually a speech
by someone seeking local office to work for the people,
who mill around the machines that sputtered in work
and hesitated and ah damn it threw a rod
and took the rest of the day to fix
so that the mowing was still to be done
and the one time, freeing up a frozen belt
that caught the sleeve
and the handshake forever after was left-handed.

The Job

Dock. Joe Pye. Greenbrier.
On the shaggy shoulder of Route 40
twenty strides from my uncle's house
there was a sign for a product,
a hand creme, not made anymore.
The parent company, then in soaps,
offered to pay my uncle to take it down.
He was a teenager, a stalk of passions.
I think it was twenty dollars they'd pay.
A lot of money for those afternoons.
They didn't want to advertise
something they didn't have to sell.
The hands on the sign had a rash of rust.
The brand name was pocked with rock shocks,
from kids testing their arms' aim.
They might have become baseball greats,
who knows what begins on the side of a two-lane?
Anyway, my uncle was keen for the money.
The man on the phone said it was an hour's job.
How my uncle was to get it down was left up to him.
Was this to encourage ingenuity, stick-to-itness,
a mini-lesson in American get-it-done?
Though the sign's legs were metal, he chose an ax.
Maybe he used the blunt side
or maybe he ruined the blade edge
knocking it raggedy with his hired chops.
My uncle was mother's youngest brother,
the late-in-life child of my grandmother.
Our hillside pa-chinged with the wrong chime of his chopping.

His father, my grandfather, was dead.
There was no one to offer another way
to do the job, and this was working,
the sign shuddering and bowing to the road,
his battering, the blows and their echoes,
lowering the wrinkle-free promise
until the roadside claimed nothing
and everyone on their way was on their own.

Those Summers

There was a track not twenty yards from the pool.
When the trains came by, coal trains mostly,
though there were always some boxcars,
the cement sides of the pool vibrated
and the diving board hummed.
The cla-tuck, cla-tuck, cla-tuck
of the cars thundered the same meaningless command,
repeating it like an angry father.
The pretty young moms and younger sitters shone,
oiled like well-lubed parts, lounged
in webbed chairs or propped on towels,
talking even in the clang and rage of tonnage.
But underwater was quiet, sudden dived-in silence.
The train was not there.
Could you outlast its long blocky sentence,
Pacific, Chesapeake, Southern, N&W, Ohio,
cars rocked and knocked, full with men's work?
It was still, ears stopped with the choleric blue.
But the body would not obey, craving the climb
to air, the sun-spangle diamond-shattered surface
where the loud world rushed back in with the freight
of women and girls, the glistening racket.

The Bursar's Office

There was a waist-high counter
where you waited,
for the bursars were always busy,
studying onion-skin papers
or rattling the calculators.
Totals arrived.
The Bursar's Office smelled of 3-IN-ONE oil.
The clock was big as the moon
with a pale face and black Roman numerals
and two black spear-headed hands.
Each desk behind the counter had a desktop calendar
with a number for each day
in the box that represented the day
and empty boxes at the end of the month
to make the grid come out even.
I went there, even when I had no business.
Can I help you was said.
And then one day a new lady bursar,
brown-hair, red fingernails,
took from the top drawer of her desk
a bag of strawberries, washed and capped,
big berries she must have gotten from the farmer's market,
ripe, heart-shaped berries she bit in half
even as she worked her pencil
with the other hand.
It was the season, plump berries,
and her slender fingers
lifted them to her lips,

eating, without counting,
then licking her thumb and index finger tip,
the quick pink of her tongue,
the staggering sums.

Work

What he remembered, even years later,
was an afternoon, an hour to go,
when they put down their shovels
and threw rocks at a pile
of glass jars, canning discards,
to kill the time
until the truck came for them.

He felt so bad, he says,
not finishing out the day,
that he can't hear breaking glass
without wanting that hour back
to work it fair and earn his pay.

It was a shit job with shit pay,
shovel work we were dropped off to early
and picked up from late
with the runty boss eyeing how far
we'd gotten with the hand ditching.
Why couldn't they send a machine?

But one afternoon, with hour to go,
we found a pile
of old jars, green with mold,
wedges of brown rain water
in their cloudy bottoms.
I challenged the boys to see
who could break the most.

Ha. Paid to throw our best
fast balls and sliders.
And sweet the pop
like a strike in the catcher's mitt.

Working Graveyard

Once, at the end of his shift,
he came out
and in the first slant light
the parking lot glittered
like the one time he'd seen the sea.
The machines still roared in his ears.
There'd been no breakdowns the whole night.
His sandwich in its brown bag
had warmed and the cheese melted a little.
He had eaten around midnight.
For some reason that night
the aisles between the looms
had seemed church-like
and his shift-mates like ushers
taking up the collection.
And now the morning sun
sprang off the asphalt
and he had the morning to putter
and then the afternoon to sleep.
People were leaving the parking lot,
breaking up the group slowly,
the way you do at the end of a service.

How It Was Done, White Furniture Company

> "The last piece of furniture came down the line, was worked on
> and then the line closed down behind it, and the workers in that
> section would be let go."
> — from *Closing: The Life and Death of an American Factory*

Let's say the last piece
was a chair, this product
with its slow progress
closing the plant.

The lumber, select oak,
was brought from the kiln.
Doesn't that sound like "killed"
they joked, since joking
was the best to be made of it.

And then the rough mill,
where for years they danced
the rip saw's rough waltz,
his hand to her hand, her hand
back to his, the barked plank
becoming usable.

After the wood was glued together
the workers in that area separated.

Then it was machined and the people …

Then sanded, assembled, finished.
Finished: the fine or decorative work,
the final treatment, the quality or state
of being perfected.

And then rubbed and packed,
that careful massage, that last touching
of the feet, the legs, the arms, the back.

Notch

I came into the shop quietly.
With the bright sun outside,
it was like entering a cave.
He called it a shop—
table saw, wood plane,
two walls hung with tools.
Women didn't come in here.

His back was to me,
something broken on the workbench.
He was singing, almost a croaking,
old frog-throat gear screaking
something something Red River Valley.
He swayed a little who never danced,
the man who was model of how to be a man.
I backed out into the blinding sun
and never told him I heard him sing.

The Ladder

He worked years on the tablet,
deciphering the pictographs. He knew
it was a kind of language, those images.
An eye. A bird, maybe a crow.
A basket of wheat. A ladder.
Did the order of the images matter?
He cross-referenced similar texts.
He studied the history of the region
and satisfied many hours in the tablet's service.
In a cousin language, a ladder
was the word for happiness, to rise up,
to be lifted above the ordinary.
After years of work, he sorted it out.
It was poetry, bad poetry, adolescent:
"Today, I am happy,
happy all this day, today."

The Gospel of the Gospel

And the prophet said: "Let not your heart
dwell in sadness, but be glad in the day."
The word used for heart has two translations:
One is as a door through which a blue sky
over whitewashed stone steps can be glimpsed
and the other has to do with a kind of clearing
in a forest of hemlock and white pine.
Sadness references the turning-inward look
of a shy child in a roomful of strangers.
Glad has a connotation of the same weight
and earthiness of certain flower bulbs
that can lie dormant or be transported
great distances in their dry drowse
and then brought to blossom when replanted.
The phrase in the day is a guess, but a good guess,
given that time passed then as now.

Acknowledgments

Thanks to the editors and readers of the magazines where the following poems first appeared.

Appalachian Heritage: "Raking"

The Atlantic Monthly: "The Ladder"

Crab Orchard Review: "Those Summers"

Crazyhorse: "Where I'm Coming From"

Field: "The Collection" and "The Song"

Iron Mountain Review: "Amen to the Ax"

Massachusetts Review: "The Gospel of the Gospel"

New Ohio Review: "The Call" and "The Elements Will Have their Way"

Poetry Daily: "The Stairs"

Southern Cultures: "Flip"

Southern Poetry Review: "Blast Mat," "The Patterns," and "Sweeping"

Threepenny Review: "The Stairs" and "The Way of the World"

TriQuarterly: "Finish Work"

Western Humanities Review: "The Job" and "Lull"

Gratitude, as always, to Michael McFee, whose careful reading helped the individual poems and the collection as a whole.

Other books from Tupelo Press

See our complete backlist at www.tupelopress.org.

CPSIA information can be obtained
at www.ICGtesting.com
Printed in the USA
FFOW05n0216180914